My Heart Is A Pen

Of A Ready Writer

(A Second Time Around)

Patricia A . Jacobs

Copyright

My Heart Is A Pen

Of A Ready Writer

(A Second Time Around)

By
Patricia A . Jacobs

Ephesians 6 :10

3

Table of Contents

Page No.

Table of Contents

Page No.

Words of Encouragement

To be thankful for what I had

To recognize my Blessings

To always keep going forward

To keep trusting God

From my Spiritual Mother - To be strong in the Lord and in the power of his might. Ephesians 6 :10

To God Be The Glory

Introduction

My Heart Is A Pen Of A Ready Writer
(A Second Time Around) , derived from
my previous book that was called My Mind
is a pen of a ready writer , that was lost to a
flash drive error during the spring of 2013.
Not being able to retrieve my writings of a
year work , I was determined to start over ,
but this time I wrote the things down that
was concerning my spiritual walk and the
things that were overflowing from within
my heart . So I decided that this book would
be called My heart Is A Pen Of A Ready
Writer (A Second Time Around) .
Sometimes my writings would stop and start
but there was always a yearning within me
to see the end results of completing a task
that God had given to me , that would
somehow make a difference or to help
someone else to stay strong in the Lord and
in the power of his might .
                                    Thanks Be To God

Chapter One

Things of the Heart

As we learn life lessons we learn in bits and peices , seeing the end process of our starting point and even then sometimes having to restart afresh , by asking God to forgive us of our sins. God desire is that we grow to know him in our hearts with a heart to know God in our spirit and in our praise. To be filled with the word is to eat it for it is good for the mind , body, soul and spirit. That is our walk with God staying strong feeding on the word daily in our hearts at all time, it's healthy and it brings about change in your life. We see the outside of a person all in order , dressed up from top to bottom and we can describe them in every way we can from their outer appearance . It is so easy to see me in front of you yet still you don't know me . You see my heart is a pen of a ready writer with thoughts even I can hardly express and explain . Sometimes

we look at the things that are in front of us
as being the very best there is , and we
loose focus on the idea that God always
have the best in store for us . I know that
God is working all this out for my good and
in my favor . Not for what I think I want ,
but for his will for me because he can see
farther than I can , Matthew 9 : 15 states
And Jesus said unto them , Can the children
of the bride chamber mourn , as long as the
bridegroom is with them ? but the days will
come , when the bridegroom shall be taken
from them , and then shall they fast . After
reading the scripture my heart was
introduced to faith and my faith was
strengthen even the more because I do
believe in and on the word of God . You see
Jesus heard my cry and turned around and
said , daughter , its alright , I hear you , so
be of good courage , I will take care of you
just stand in peace that your faith in me will
be strengthened even the more , for I am still
in control , and I replied ok ,Yes Lord ,I
will . It's good to know the Lord for he is

good and I am an over comer of my past .
Thank you Father for a new beginning for
the past is behind me , and a greater future is
before me , because I desire better than
yesterday . I want to live and not die in my
living .I see my life in a position with Gods
words like never before . I glanced back at
my life and how I used to respond to
situations and then I realized that God had
took those obstacles and reactions away
from me .They were suddenly gone in a
twinkling of an eye. The old in me had been
taken away because of my heart desire to be
free . I do believe that we can try so hard to
only recognize that our time isn't Gods time
because God has a set time for us to achieve
the purpose and goals that he has for us. I've
looked forward to seeing destiny unfold
before me so many times. I thought my time
was at hand and I could taste the winners
line of victory before me . Sometimes my
strength dwindles and I find myself gaining
new strength through calling on God and his
word. When you walk this road with Father

You will find that your life will never be the same as you learn of him. Unusual things are beginning to happen to me . Things are happening to me when I speak in line with God word and in the authority that he has given to me. The Lord opened my eyes and showed me my own heart then I began to walk in a willingness to be obedient before him. Speak Lord for my spirit is at peace knowing that you are in control . The Holy Spirit spoke to me and asked can you wait on the Lord , at first I was amazed at the voice because the words were so clear . I was slow to answer and it caused me to think for a second , I smiled and said yes I can wait because my desire is to be kept by God .There is no one as important to me than God is . I am to hold on to my dreams because I'm too close to let go. As children God gives us a Father an earthly man to be there for us and to take care of our needs , and as we grow in the word we began to see God as our Heavenly Father who is bigger than man , and who can do exceedingly and

11

marvelous things far more than we can ever imagine . I decided that while I'm waiting on Father that am just going to be strong in the Lord and in the power of his might . God has this and all things in his hand . Amen .To God be the Glory. Jesus said that I could do all things with him . Then a question comes to me . Can you do all things with Jesus ? Yes I can because Jesus lives within me . I am looking to live in the overflow having the windows of Heaven to open upon me and in my life. I yearn for Father to hold me in his arm for security and safety. I also want to see a little light a little light to open my heart and fill me with joy forevermore . For theirs no where to go and know one to go to because I desire greater and victory is for me . God is so amazing at feeding our souls when our heart is ready to receive what he has to offer us. My heart has been so overwhelmed with thanksgiving unto God for being my everything , for being the I Am in my life ,and for being the God of whom ever I need him to be. One night I called a family member for prayer and my hopes was for them to go to God right then for a miracle on my behalf . You see prayer is the most important thing in my life that a person can do for me because I know in my heart that when one is praying for me that there prayer will cover every aspect of my life . The word says that the prayers of the righteous availed much . God is so good and all of my hope is in him . God sits high and looks low for he is able to do all things above all that we could ever imagine. Father hears me when I call him d fulfills my need of peace to a place of safety. Father removes me from the storms and out of the storms of life. I surrender to my Lord and Savior . My soul says here am I Lord cover me in your arms . Although at times I do get weary , but I can't give up .Giving up is not an option for me , for this is not my battle , it's the Lords. The trails come and blow before me , yet I stand and continue to call on God . I seek Father throughout the day and night for a longing to be in a place of peace . Early in the morning I ask the Holy Spirit to lead and guide me in truth , and as Father prepares the day for me, I have to seek God, that my way be made prosperous . Then I ask the Holy Spirit to move me out of the way and have his way. Father I need your spirit living in me and without you I am lost . I surrender again as I call on the spirit of the living God to live inside of me , for in my weakness God is made strong , for great is his faithfulness . People change , life changes , we go and we come . Yet again there is nothing new under the sun. For God is the same today tomorrow and he will be the same forever , for he never changes .

Chapter Two

From the Bible to Me

When Paul and Silas began to pray ,
afterwards they began to sing and an
earthquake began to shake and to move the
foundation on which they were standing .
Look at the mighty works of God acting on
our behalf when we are obedient to the word
of God . As I began to study a little
concerning Paul , I see Paul with a thorn in
his side that had a grip on him , and God
said my grace is sufficient for thee , for my
strength is made perfect in weakness . God
is able to keep us , in whatever state that we
are in . A close friend was in need of some
necessities and I wasn't in the position to
help them . All I could do was to go in
prayer to God on their behalf . On the
following day , they said that there prayers
were answered and I thanked God for
hearing and answering our prayers , for
prayer changes things . I was told that

manna will not be falling from Heaven anymore , but that it would be coming to us by the way of God touching mans heart towards each other . I also heard that the word now is taking place at this very moment .The scripture states in the book of Hebrew 11: 1 Now faith is the substance of things hoped for the evidence of things not seen . It's the faith that we hath to believe for at the moment . Not the next minute , the next hour , nor tomorrow , but right now . It is Right Now .Then I heard about the table in Psalm 23 , that there's a table that the Lord has prepared for me in the presence of my enemies and there's nothing that the enemy can do about it , because what God has for me is for me , including his goodness and mercy . As I listened to the Holy Spirit speak to my spirit continuously about the sermon on the eagle I began to ask God for more wisdom , knowledge and for more understanding of the message as to the things that were going on in my life . The answer for me was to make a choice to stand in strength or to stand in weakness . So I began to gain strength and courage by the way of the word and realizing that first I must know how to stand on my own two feet . Then I began to feast on the word even the more with an understanding still realizing that my heart is to be cleansed from the inner man . Standing like an eagle has brought me through some tough winds . Winds in which I had to command to be still in the name of Jesus. One evening our church was invited to another church and the Pastor was preaching from the book of Isaiah Chapter 6: 1. It was then that I could see God given me more understanding and confirmation as to what I was going through in my life. My mother was the first one to ever introduce me to the word confirmation . She would say that when the word or message is being spoken to me the second time , that it seals and bonds what God is speaking to me .The pastor went on to say that sometimes God hath to shift things around in our lives , to get our attention focused on him , for us to get to know who he is and for us to give him the glory . My soul began to get happy and to rejoice because I was hearing the voice of God speaking his word to me , that he created all things and that all things belong to him . Now I see David as I entered the cave of only darkness in the mist of a mind of hope . I am alone with no parents and family members are not around . I can't grab onto my Mother to hear her say to read Psalm 23 nor can I call my Father to hear him say to me , baby it's alright just stay in Gods hand , he will take care of you . While in the cave , it seems as though there is no outlet and sometimes you want to cry out in a loud voice , but who's going to hear you when the cave doors are closed and the shadow of light is too dim to see . Then I feel myself getting hungry and I go to the pantry of my heart and feast on the word that I had gathered along the way . I eat with a spirit of hope on the inside that I will be filled and my prayers answered . Sometimes

I grab onto just enough word to get me from one minute to the next . When I eat the word it doesn't always taste good because of the choices that I have made . Time has a position and a length but God is always in control . As we take a glance at the book of 11 Kings 20: 1- 6 we see how Isaiah the prophet , went to Hezekiah with a message from God telling him to get his house in order , that he was going to die , so Hezekiah began to pray in heaviness of heart to God asking God to remember how he had lived his life . When Isaiah left from being with Hezekiah the Lord spoke to him with a message for Hezekiah , when Isaiah returned to Hezekiah , he told him that God had heard his cry and that he had added fifteen more years of living to his life , see how much more God has in store for us. In stillness I ask the Holy Spirit to take over my flesh because my flesh is constantly trying to make decisions for me and therefore it battles against my spirit . That's why it is so important to have the word in your heart and to be constantly fed with the word of God . As I sat in the cave , I yearn for a touch of the masters hand upon me . The tears that are flowing come running down warm onto my face . They are sometimes so hard to stop flowing so I ask father to open the doors then I began to feel and see Gods grace and mercy upon me . I still see David in the cave , as he is talking to God about everything . You see David had a lot going on in his past and present living and I can imagine when he longed for the minute , just a minute to have peace in his mind , body , soul and spirit . And Joseph , Joseph had to sit in a pit and to travel through some obstacle courses until he became governor of the land . One Sunday the pastor preached about being on the mountain top , and it is truly a wonderful place to be , but we hath to come back down to the world , back to reality just as Moses did . What a place of rest and peace just to be on the mountain top with Father . To feel his presence and to have his spirit resting on you . Blesseth be the name of the Lord , for he is worthy to be praised . As I take a glimpse at the Queen , Queen Esther and how she reached out to touch the kings sceptre , and then I see my Father Jesus as he shows his favor upon me .Then I thought back to the book of Job , about all of his trails and health issues . But look at God , my Healer and Restorer . Jobs later was greater than his beginning , for he was blessed with more than he had at first and so shall my later be as well. Father I'm in a dry land and the people are crying out for your help. As I began to pray to Father , I asked God to give me a word and to bless me to be a help to someone . A close friend began to express what the doctors had said concerning them and they began to speak in faith how their family had come together in prayer and I mentioned the saying about generational curses , how we hath to bind them up in the name of Jesus . They then mentioned , turning their plate down and believing that God is able to move on the things that they were in prayer for . My response was , well I can do the same because I to believe . And I know that God had already worked out a blessing for them that was already in the making. Because of our faith it's already done. The word states that weeping my endure for a night but joy cometh in the morning , you see , we don't know when our morning is coming , but it's coming , so we wait with an expectancy that God will deliver in his time . During the times that I'm waiting for my break through I say Lord I thank you that your timing is what's best for me , that you're taking care of me , your child . As I continue to wait , I know within my heart that God has something good and much greater for me . Remember when Isaac saw his Father Abraham with the fire and the wood , Isaac said where is the Lamb for the burnt offering , and Abraham , knowing in his heart what he was about to do , said my son God will provide . Even today God is still providing and supplying our everyday

needs .God is good and we all need help ,
like Moses , he couldn't uphold himself in
battle so Aaron and Hur held him up on each
side while the battle was being won . And
Jonah , have you ever had a Jonah
experience in that you were being
disobedient and you found yourself making
the wrong choice , wanting to do things
your way . Then you sit and try to reason
within yourself to make sense out of what
you had done only to realize that you are
being chastised by the Lord. At this point
you admit to God that you were wrong and
ask Father to forgive you of your sins , as
you have been forgiven , now you can go
and sin no more . I thank God for given me a
second chance to get it right and to make
better choices. As a friend was given me
some spiritual advice , I was told to be
humble , be still and to praise God. They
mentioned to me how we are broken to
pieces and that God is able to put us back
together even better than before, like the
potters vessels . As I began to speak and cry

out to God I found myself in total worship
that took over my thoughts , will and desire.
I had entered into Gods rest and peace .
Even laying down worshipping God and
awakening in a worshipping spirit . What a
beautiful experience it is to rest in the arms
of God . During church services one Sunday
the visiting Pastor began to preach his
sermon on Worship. He explained what
worship was and how vital it was to ask the
Holy Spirit to come and dwell within you.
He also talked about how one is to worship
God which is in spirit and in truth . As he
continued he gave scriptures out for us to
see for ourselves for what the word says
about worship and that we are to come to the
house of worship being already , ready to
receive a word from God , having the Holy
Spirit in us . As I have taken in new
information my mind and heart has also
been renewed with more understanding of
the word worship. Hearing the sermon on
worship has truly made me to reverence the
Holy Spirit even more and to see God as

being the awesome God that he is. Just like
the lady who went to the well ,God had
positioned her to be still and to wait for
Jesus arrival . For God knows everything ,
as he told his disciples earlier , I must need
to go to Samaria but at the time the disciples
didn't understand why their travels were
being changed so , just like the disciples we
have asked the Lord why am I going here or
why am I doing this or that . Remember that
there is nothing new under the sun . As with
the Samaritan woman she received her
season of blessings from Jesus and she had
received new life with living water that she
would never thirst again for anything
because she excepted the true and living
word of God from God . So it was at the
well that her whole life was changed and
blessed by God . As I lay down and began to
talk to God , and the story of the lady that
was brought to the court before men came to
my spirit and it reminded me of our own
hearts towards each other . I can imagine
seeing the lady standing all alone before the

town with her head hanging down as she's
in prayer to God with a repentant heart .
Then I see Jesus coming to her side to
rescue her from a circle of people who was
about to stone her . Have you ever been in
that kind of position in which the people
were about to stone you and Jesus said he
that is without sin , cast the first stone. As I
take a step back and look into my heart I'm
asking God to give me a pure heart and to
remove everything out of and away from my
heart that is not like him. Then I take a look
at my hands and ask God to fill them with
his touch and with his healing. Sometimes
my mind reflect back to the lady with the
issue of blood and how great a desire she
had to just touch the helm of Jesus garment.
Just maybe she saw the anointing that
surrounded Jesus as he walked about or just
suppose she saw her break through and
wondered , well I can't touch his face , his
hands , so I'll just keep crawling towards
him enough to reach out and touch the end
of his garment , for of a surety he is clean

and that the anointing is on his clothing as well. There has been a lot of times that I have cried out and that I have said that if I could just touch the helm of his garment, that I would be made whole . What a powerful statement in itself.

Chapter Three

Gods Will For Me

Through my life and in my life , God has always been with me , inspite of the choices and situations that I've made in my life . The newest chapter in my life began when I received deliverance from my own will to excepting Gods will for my life, because I now know that Gods will is what's best for me. To God be the Glory. As I look back I'm realizing more that God has already planned my life in the plan that he has for me. Letting go and letting God positions me to want to live in Gods will .Submission to God gives me great peace. God has a will for all of us in his timing. While you're in submission to Gods will, you go through a change, a process of cleansing and pruning of the heart and the mind until we come in right standing with God and his words . It may take a day , a month , a year or even a life time , but through it all , you'll gain closeness , faith , trust and more strength in God. You will also begin to seek God and his desire for you . As I walk through this life I found myself walking and talking to God as I faced the issues of life that surrounded me. Walking with only the word the true word of God . You see the word has and is my I Am .God is good to me. As I lay down to rest, I rest with an expectancy to hear from God , and the Holy Spirit would speak to me and I would begin writing , not just writing , but under the anointing of the Holy Spirit . As I write my spirit is speaking to God from the must inner part of my soul . My soul yearns and thirsts after God. No other help I have and know, for God is my provider , my keeper , and my everything. God is a faithful and a just God .For he loves us more than we could ever imagine within ourselves. Seek God and do good . For the joy of the Lord is my strength for Gods words gives me new hope, that takes me through the day as I stand on his promises . I have found love and peace in God , for he is Holy . He has heard my cry again and he is still keeping my soul in quietness and in stillness. As I was talking to Father , I began to say Lord am always talking to you and right now Father I need a word from you .As I began to be still , Fathers words came to me , to be stedfast and unmovable , always abounding in the work of the Lord . After I had received the word , I thanked God and then I went to the Bible to find the scripture which was in 1 Corinthians 15 : 58 ,and the ending of the scripture said , Now yea not that the work of the Lord that is in you is not in vain . Gods words are so powerful and to the human mind , it is just amazing . During a Sundays service the Pastors sermon was on power and that we are first to believe and that we are to take limits off of God because God is a big God . Of course there was more encouraging words and scriptures. The following morning Gods words to me was to work on me , myself , to get me right .I'm continuing to take one day at a time and not look at the cares of tomorrow, although sometimes the cares have overtaken me, to the point where as my God comes to rescue me to victory .I remember a time when I had asked God for a special blessing , but I asked in faith , knowing that God would honor my prayer in his will , and he heard my prayer and delivered. My level of faith increased when I began to take on trusting in the word of God . I'm beginning to hear what thus saith the Lord. God is our help and our refuge in times of trouble. When theirs tumult and a restless spirit God is able to come in and turn everything around when we are focused on his words . I am determined to stand strong on the word of God . I have a strong desire on the inside to follow God and to seek his face .God knows my heart and I want Gods will and desires for me. As I look at my life I see things that are not in place as I think they should be. I said as I think they should be , and the only avenue or resource that I have is the word of

31

God . Last year was truly a year of faith , trust and spiritual growth for me because throughout last year I was faced with some trails , that only God could have brought me out of. Each trail has strengthened my trust and faith in God .I have always had a hunger on the inside of me that kept me chasing after God. A hunger and a desire for the word ,that leads me to go searching for direction that's going to put me in right standing with God. There has been many mornings where as I have asked God to move me out of his way and to have me to be the willing vessel to speak his word and to position me to receive a word in doing so. I thank God for putting his people and children in my path. I have been talked to and in some instances I'm sure that I have been corrected as well. Then as I see the new year approaching I heard the sermon on My cup runneth over, and the scripture from Matthew 6 :33 was mentioned . It stated But seek ye first the kingdom of God , and his righteousness; and all these things shall be added unto you. Immediately I knew that was the answer that I needed to hear . I had been seeking God , but mostly for his hand , when I should have been more focused on seeking Gods heart . As the year is coming to an end I see it as now being complete . I truly thank God for bringing me through it all only to see a new year in seeking more of who he is .

Chapter Four

Being Still

Where do I begin .Test and trails come to make me strong and that my ending will be greater than my beginnings. My life began long ago but I didn't really begin to live until I started , no not me , but when God began to do his work of molding , shaping and making me over to his will . Even in my trails and situations I began to grab onto God in faith and just holding on to the fact that he has the last say so and what the devil had for bad God has already made it for my good .Through my trails and my struggles I had to speak the word to myself and to circumstances that were beyond my control . When the trails of life come your way how will you respond? Who do you call on to talk to? As for me there were questions that I didn't have the answers to. As I was going through my trails, words came to me to only

talk to God , meaning don't give the devil
the satisfaction of words to be strolled
through and about . You see the chapters of
my life is rolling by and I see the years come
in and go out . We take the past , and we
learn from it . Past experiences is a good
teacher , for out of the past comes
testimonies , testimonies to help someone
else to get through what we have already
been through , and your past makes you
stronger , especially when you're walking
with the Lord on your side . Walking in
purpose , being humble and trusting God
makes life path way a little clearer. Then I
thought back to manna from Heaven
and I see how God fed the people in the
wilderness . And today I'm seeing God feed
me and how he is supplying all of my needs
even when I'm on my last . Amazing things
of God working in my life, very exciting
things and all I have to do is to stay in
alignment with Gods word. This is truly a
time of harvest and a land of plenty. The
previous year I saw what I had as being little

but it was actually a blessing because
I didn't know that I would have had the
things that I did have. During that time I
began to take on a mighty grateful heart to
everything that came my. Everything is
plenty and is more than enough. The time of
harvest is overflowing , and my cup running
over . To God be the glory. I am overcoming
all of those past obstacles that had been
holding me down , because of an increase in
my level of faith . And I am believing that
God is bringing me into his garden , into the
land of plenty , in the name of Jesus Christ ,
my Lord and Savior. Usually when I awaken
and go into prayer , I would open the Bible
to the book of Psalm for a word from the
Lord , but this particular morning I had a
thirst for the living word , a thirst , as if I
was ordering from a food menu , knowing
exactly what I needed to quench my thirst
and appetite . A true thirst that would fill my
spirit , a thirst that filled me with strength in
knowing that whatsoever I was to do , I
would succeed and prosper in it. That was

truly a word of assurance that I needed to
hold on to, because it will come to pass in
due time, in my season . Greater , yes
greater is coming to me today . I am to
speak in authority for God is not a man that
he should lie. I declare and decree that
greater is coming , it is here , for the
Blessings of Abraham is upon me. The
words exclaims that greater is he that is in
me than he that is in the world . Even as I
look back on my life, I give all the credit to
God and his word . I made it through and
I'm still traveling , just with a different mind
set , because my mind has been renewed and
my mind is made up to continue to follow
Jesus . During this point in time , there was a
great storm in the area . I will admit that
seeing the rain and winds and the panic on
the face of the people , I was a bit moved.
But then I begin to pray for peace in the rain
and in the winds. Suddenly as I continued to
drive I began to see a picture of peace in the
path that I was traveling . When I got home I
received a call from a family member telling

me how the storm was in the area that they were in, and how they had to weather the storm . They then asked me if I had ever weathered a storm . I replied and responded yes and I went on to explain as to how the weather was in the area that I had just traveled in. Then I began to think about the raining of situations and the strong winds of life that was trying to surround me . In my heart I know that they are trails and that I have to take what I was going through as a growth process to prepare me to be the person for the job that God has in store for me . As time is going on I am beginning to have a different prayer voice with great expectations and as the days are going by I'm seeing the hand of God pouring back into my life and restoring things that the devil stole from me, but I'm receiving double portions in an abundance ,with a heart of gratefulness and thanksgiving to God . Sometimes my soul gets so happy that tears begin to flow. They are tears of thanksgiving and a humble heart for all that

God has done and is doing for me . In such need of an ending to endless tears and hurt , I ask God to come into my mind , body ,soul and spirit . For God will wipe our tears away and take away sadness to give joy and must of all we hath to know that God is the I Am to whatever we need him to be. When Moses was about to depart from talking to God , before returning back to the children of Israel , Moses said whom shall I say has sent me , and God replied , in Exodus 3 : 14 I Am hath sent you. For God is all knowing , and he knows the intent of the heart , for he created us .So I'm to rejoice , and let God have his way and to fret not for God said that weeping may endure for a night , but joy cometh in the morning . As I began to be still , the tears began to stop flowing and to start to disappear . Even through my tears , I've learned that tears are a cleansing tool , a pouring out of and letting go of worries and cares of this world . The release of tears refreshes us with a sigh of relief , for God catches all of our tears in a bottle and

attends to our every cry to prepare us for
newness. Sometimes you hath to speak over
yourself the word of God. You hath to know
who God is and that God is the creator of
everything . After grasping onto being still ,
I had to have a heart check. When God
chastises us our eyes begin to see within our
heart , so clear that our sin will be brought to
the forefront of our mind . It's like the
removing of blindfolds away from your
eyes . The covers are being removed and the
true you is revealed . Therefore God will
step in with favor to rescue us in the time of
trouble . My job and task is to be still and
wait on God . Even as I'm waiting I am to
watch , pray and catch up on a start to a new
beginning , which is a life to live for God ,
whom I will seek after , for the best is yet to
come. I have to be still and ask Father to be
my guide all through the day and night and
for his peace to take over me for I do
surrender unto him. Peace be still. I have
also been asking the Holy spirit to move me
out of the way so that I could hear from

God. I'm always talking to God never being still enough at times to hear what God wants to tell me. This particular morning I received a scripture to read , to record in my journal along with a song , afterwards I began to sit still, not even dwelling on anything and the Holy Spirit spoke to me and said Who is man that thou art mindful of him and the son of man that thou visited him . I understood in a quickness that God was speaking to my spirit and immediately I began to search the scripture out for more understanding and the ending of the scripture continued to read as , Oh Lord Our Lord how excellent is thy name in all the earth . To God be the glory and my spirit leaped with joy.

Chapter Five

My Prayer to God

Oh Lord my Lord , how excellent is thy name in all the earth . Father please forgive me of my sins and Lord I thank you , are some of the words of expression that arises when I open my mouth to talk to God because he has truly been good to me . Father I surrender all to you, my mind , body, soul and spirit , endow me with your Holy spirit , filling me with divine wisdom and knowledge . Empty me out Father that I may be filled with joy and peace and to have more of you for the work that you have for me . I am yours Lord lead me and guide me in the way that I am to go. Lord order my speech that even my thoughts will be in order before you in correctness . Father guide my thoughts that I may record your wonderful works of blessings and miracles in my life. Words can't express how awesome you are . I am so thankful to God for everything that he has done for me and for what he is about to do for me . Gods words have put my life in a new direction. Thank you Father for this appointed time in my life. Thank you Father for comforting me, for you said that you would never leave me nor forsake me. For you will forever be with me, at all times. Thank you Father for bringing me from such long ways, for all the ways of kindness , and for the Holy Spirit speaking to my spirit to want to have a transformed mind to do your will . Your words have brought much change to my heart in my daily living. For when I was in need of direction you taught me to be still and to listen to your words. In a silent and quite voice God said to me to speak into the atmosphere , speak those things as though they were , to be strong in the Lord and in the power of his might , and to see spiritually , no longer am I to see things in the natural , but to see with my spiritual eyes. In your word you said that we would understand it better by and by for your grace is sufficient and your favor is everlasting . Still standing , but now I'm standing with a smile because I heard a word from the Lord in Isaiah 51; 1-3 Hearken to me , ye that follow after righteousness , ye that seek the Lord ; look unto the rock whence ye are hewn , and to the hole of the pit whence ye are digged. Look unto Abraham your father , and Sara that bare you: for I called him alone , and blessed him , and increased him. For the Lord shall comfort Zion ; he will comfort all her waste places ; and he will make her wilderness like Eden , and her desert like the garden of the Lord ; joy and gladness shall be found therein thanksgiving and the voice of melody.

Chapter Six

Speak Life into Yourself

Now that the year is ending and a new year is approaching , the Holy Spirit is speaking new and greater things into my life and into my spirit , such as seeking God first , to believe and have faith, to stop putting limits on what God can do and to see God as a Mighty God. To speak in authority , to declare and decree things into my life , to be of good courage , to be determined to see the end results and to use the gifts that God has put into my hands.

Greater Things - Great is the Lord , and greatly to be praised ; and his greatness is unsearchable
Psalm 145 : 3

Seeking God - But seek ye first the kingdom of God , and his righteousness : and all these things shall be added unto you.
Matthew 6 :33

Believe - Therefore I say unto you , What things so ever ye desire , when ye pray , believe that ye receive them , and ye shall have them.
Mark 11:24

Faith - Now faith is the substance of things hoped for , the evidence of things not seen.
Hebrews 11:1

No limits - I can do all things through Christ which strengthen me.
Philippians 4 : 13

A Mighty God - Who is this King of Glory The Lord strong and mighty , the Lord mighty in battle.
Psalm 24 : 8

Authority - For he taught them as one having authority , and not as the scribes.
Matthew 7 : 29

To Declare and Decree - One generation shall praise thy works to another , and shall declare thy mighty acts .
Psalm 145 - 4

Courage - Be of good courage , and he shall strengthen your heart , all ye that hope in the Lord.
Psalm 31 :24

Being Strong - Be strong in the Lord and in the power of his might .
Ephesians - 6 :10

Strength - The Lord is my strength and song, and he is my God , and I will prepare him an habitation , my father's God , and I will exalt him.
Exodus 15 :2

47

Gifts - A man's gift maketh room for him, and bringeth him before great men.
Proverbs 18 : 16

Wisdom - If any of you lack wisdom , let him ask of God ,that giveth to all men liberally , and upbraideth not ; and it shall be given him,
James 1:5

Chapter Seven

Scriptures to Grow on for Strength

Exodus 15: 2
The Lord is my strength and song , and he is my God , and I will prepare him an inhabitation , my father's God , and I will exalt him.

2 Samuel 22: 33
God is my strength and power : and he maketh my way perfect.

Psalm 23:1
The Lord is my shepherd : I shall not want.

Psalm 24:1-5
(1). The earth is the Lord's , and the fullness thereof : the world , and they that dwell therein.

(2). For he hath founded it upon the seas ,
and established it upon the floods.
(3). Who shall ascend into the hill of the
Lord ? Or who shall stand in his holy place?
(4). He that hath clean hands , and a pure
heart : who hath not lifted up his soul unto
vanity , nor sworn deceitfully.
(5). He shall receive the blessing from the
Lord , and righteousness from the God of his
salvation.

Psalm 27: 1-2
(1).The Lord is my light and my salvation :
whom shall I fear ?
(2)The Lord is the strength of my life : of
whom shall I be afraid?

Psalm 28:7
The Lord is my strength and my shield : my
heart trusted in him , and I am helped :
therefore my heart greatly rejoiceth ; and
with my song will I praise him.

Psalm 46:1

GOD is our refuge and Strength , a very present help in trouble.

Psalm 62: 1-2

(1). Truly my soul waited upon God : from him cometh my salvation.

(2). He only is my rock and my salvation: he is my defence : I shall not be greatly moved.

Psalm 91:1-4

(1). He that dwelleth in the secret place of the most High , shall abide under the shadow of the Almighty.

(2). I will say of the Lord , He is my refuge and my fortress : my God : in him will I trust,

(3). Surely he shall deliver thee from the snare of the fowler , and from the noisome pestilence .

(4). He shall cover thee with his feathers , and under his wings shalt thou trust : his truth shall be thy shield and buckler.

Psalm 121: 1-8

(1).A song of degrees . I will lift up mine eyes unto the hill , from whence cometh my help.

(2). My help cometh from the Lord , which made heaven and earth.

(3). He will not suffer thy foot to be moved : he that keepeth thee will not slumber .

(4). Behold , he that keepeth Israel shall neither slumber nor sleep.

(5). The Lord is thy keeper: the Lord is thy shade upon thy right hand.

(6). The sun shall not smite thee. By day , nor the moon by night.

(7) .The Lord shall preserve thee from all evil: he shall preserve thy soul.

(8) .The Lord shall preserve thy going out and thy coming in from this time forth , and even for evermore.

Isaiah 40: 29

He giveth power to the faint: and to them

that have no might he increaseth strength .

Matthew 6: 33
But seek ye first the kingdom of God , and his righteousness ; and all these things shall be added unto you.

John 3: 16
For God so Loved the world, that he gave his only begotten Son, that whosoever believeth in him should not perish, but have everlasting life.

Ephesians 5: 1
Be ye followers of God , as dear children

Hebrews 11: 6
But without faith it is impossible to please him, for he that cometh to God must believe that he is a rewarder of them that diligently seek him.

Philippians 1: 6
Being confident of this very thing , that he

which hath begun a good work in you will perform it until the day of Jesus Christ.

1 Peter 2:24
Who his own self bare our sins in his own body on the tree, that we , being dead to sins , should live unto righteousness : by whose stripes ye were healed .

Philippians 4: 19
But my God shall supply all your need according to his riches in glory by Christ Jesus.

Matthew 5: 16
Let your light so shine before men, that they may see your good works , and glorify your Father which is in heaven.

Chapter Eight

Five Steps To Heaven

1. <u>Step One </u>is to acknowledge that you have sinned.
"As it is written , there is none righteous no, not one".
Romans 3:10
"For All have sinned , and come short of the glory of God".
Romans 3:23

2. <u>Step Two </u>is to realize that there is a penalty for your sin.
"For the wages of sin is death…"
Romans 6 :23 a
The word "death" means separation . The death referred to here means eternal separation from God into the lake of fire as stated in
Revelation 21:8.
"But the fearful , and unbelieving, and the abominable , and murderers ,and

whoremongers , and sorcerers, and idolaters, and all liars , shall have their part in the lake which burneth with fire and brimstone: which is the second death."
Revelation 21:8

3. Step Three is to acknowledge that Christ paid the penalty of sin for you. "But God commendeth his love toward us, in that, while we were yet sinners ,Christ died for us."
Romans 5 :8

4. Step Four is to acknowledge that Christ wants to give you the free gift of eternal life in heaven.
"... but the gift of God is eternal life through Jesus Christ our Lord."
Romans 6:23 b

5. Step Five is that you must believe in Christ and ask Him to be your Savior.
"That if thou shalt confess with thy mouth the Lord Jesus , and shalt believe in thine

heart that God hath raised him from the dead
, thou Shalt BE SAVED ."

Romans 10:9
"For with the heart man believeth unto
righteousness ; and with the mouth
confession is made unto salvation."
Romans 10:10
For whosoever shall call upon the name of
the Lord shall be saved."
Romans 10:13

Chapter Nine

Chapters in Review

Chapter One - Things of the Heart expresses the
inward thoughts of my heart.

Chapter Two - From the Bible to Me takes a look at
some people and places in the bible and how they
were strengthened and blessed through their trails
and tribulations .

Chapter Three - Gods Will For Me positioned me to
submit to him , to let go and let God.

Chapter Four - Being Still taught me to be humbled
before God.

Chapter Five - My Prayer to God speaks of my
relationship and conversation with God .

Chapter Six - Speak Life into Yourself is a list of
scriptures that changed my speech with new
motivation and guidance in seeing greater things .

Chapter Seven - Scriptures to Grow On reminds me
of who God is.

Chapter Eight - Five Steps to Heaven which gives
you an invitation to eternal life.

Chapter Nine - Gives a brief summary of all the
chapters.

Chapter Ten - A Word Of Hope

Chapter 10
A Word Of Hope
Hope

Honour the Lord with thy substance , and with the first fruits of all thine increase .
Proverbs 3 : 9

O Lord our Lord , how excellent is thy name in all the earth ! **Psalm 8 : 9**

PRAISE ye the Lord . O give thanks unto the Lord ; for he is good ; for his mercy endureth for ever. **Psalm 106 : 1**

Every word of God is pure : he is a shield unto them that put their trust in him.
Proverbs 30 : 5

Job 14 : 7
For there is hope of a tree , if it be cut down , that it will sprout again , and that the tender branch thereof will not cease.

Where there is Hope
There is Power

Hebrews 11: 1 Now faith is the substance of things hoped for , the evidence of things not seen .

Ephesians 6 : 10

Finally , my brethen, be strong in the Lord, and in the power of his might.